A STUDY

A STUDY SKILLS GUIDE

INTRODUCTION TO WRITTEN SUBJECTS & STUDYING AT UNIVERSITY

Kyriacos Papasavva

YOUCAXTON PUBLICATIONS

OXFORD & SHREWSBURY

Contents

Introduction

It is the hope of every good teacher that his or her pupils become independent learners; more capable and inquisitive and develop a love of learning that will enable the student to surpass the basic academic requirements of an institution – whatever they may be – and instead, as an individual, fall in love with all subjects as well as the subject of choice. In this hope, there is also a realisation: a teacher is, in many ways, nothing more than a facilitator; one who opens doors of knowledge, and through example, encouragement and teacherly love inspires the love of learning.

Different students are at different stages on the road to becoming independent learners. This book is aimed at those students who have not yet wholly completed this transition, yet find themselves in a place that requires its existence; university is such a place.

At university there is an immediate need for students to know the answers to questions surrounding pedagogy i.e. how one can learn *best*. The explicit understanding of this is not something innate; instead, I believe, our current education system experienced by many before university, can create a student accustomed to spoon-fed learning, which often has a negative impact on student achievement at university. Obtaining a degree is in itself challenging, but it becomes more so if essential study skills are absent.

It is both in light of the above and also as a result of the Academic Study Skills Programme at Heythrop College, University of London, that I have been inspired to write this small guide. I hope my students there, those private and those in the latter stages of state education (KS5), both current and future will find this of some use.

There is a quote by John of Salisbury which for me, a truth rings ever true: 'We stand on the shoulders of giants'. I am indebted to all my teachers, who have taught me a great deal. In particular, I would like to thank Keir Crawley and Richard Price for being amongst the most inspirational individuals I have ever met within education.

I would not be able to show due gratitude to those who have made me the person I am today without also thanking my brilliant wife who encouraged me to write this short guide and for her unfailing love and support; she is the best of wives; Proverbs 31.

What to expect and what attitude to develop

In the first year of study, it is important that students learn what is expected of them and develop the essential skills required to consistently produce good quality essays so that in the middle and final stages of written degrees, when results are more heavily weighted, students will be able to achieve their full potential. The first year, which surprises many students, is not to be seen simply as an opportunity for drinking! Instead, it is the first opportunity to learn those essential skills, which will successfully see students through subsequent years.

It is difficult to learn these essential skills later if you have not practised them during your first year of study, and this is why starting as you mean to go on is imperative. Remember that everything to do with success begins with fostering the correct mental attitude. The first step with regard to this process is *desire*; if you want it enough, work hard and you will achieve your potential.

It is important to note that the average mark students attain during their first year is usually considerably lower than in subsequent years. Most universities weight the latter years of study and the reason for this is clear: it is because the essential skills required to pass a degree are often not fully developed in the first year and sometimes non-existent; like everything else, they need to be learnt. As a result, some universities discount the first year of study altogether so that it does not count in any way towards the final degree classification and simply needs to be passed in order to attain access to the second year. In other cases, the first year counts for a marginal percentage of the overall grade, usually no more than 12%. You should enquire with your university regarding the grade weighting for each year; it is important to know, as you can use this information to accurately discern your average grade. This is especially useful if you find yourself on a borderline between grades; in such a case, you can exert yourself to attain the higher classification.

> Do not be disheartened if your grades do not match your expectations at first - a little focus, with hard work, will go a long way. Many good students in sixth form or college, who were accustomed to attaining 90% and above, are often surprised with the results they attain in their first year.

As a student, you should see your first year as an opportunity to try different approaches, and at times make mistakes when they will not count heavily against you. Thus, through a process of gradual learning, and at times through trial and error, a steady positive correlation should be evident in your marks throughout the years. When it comes to writing essays, practise literally does make perfect.

Keep in mind that an 'opportunity to make mistakes' does not mean foolishness. I will give you an example:

> When I was in my first year at university, I heard of a myth that once, in an examination, a student was asked to answer the question: 'If this were the question, what would be the answer?' To which the student wrote: 'If this were the answer, what would be the question?' He then, allegedly, walked out of the exam and received top marks. Thus, I wrote a 200 word, perfectly logical *essay*, for a question set by my lecturer, Peter Vardy, and proudly presented it to him. (The word limit was 2000 words). He read it in what felt like 10 seconds, and then looked at me with eyes of death and asked, "Where is the rest?", at which my heart sank. I tell you now, from my experience, the aforementioned myth is a lie!

In recent years, many universities have introduced study skill courses that run either shortly before or, ideally, during the course. Or, if you're very lucky, both. Engaging with these courses, especially in your first year, is an essential step on a long road that will lead to academic success; though, as with all things, not the only way. I often ask those graduates who attained the highest grades what study method they used. While their responses vary, they always show a holistic engagement with the course in every aspect; this includes attending *all* lectures, tutorials and seminars and additional trips where possible, if your university offers such activities. It might seem plainly obvious, however you would be surprised at how many students omit what they feel are non-essential elements of the course, and suffer as a result. There are no non-essential elements of your course at university; attend everything.

From my personal experience, it was only when I was sitting before my lecturers in tutorials that I really learnt how to write a good essay. If your university is one that has any of the aforementioned support, i.e. tutorials or seminars, it would be wise to take full advantage.

In fact, most universities do offer some kind of tutorial system. Better organised universities, with higher teacher-student ratios, are usually able to facilitate 1:1 tutorials between a student and a lecturer. This is a golden opportunity to increase your knowledge on the subject, as well as finding out where you went wrong and what you did well with respect to the question/s set. Other universities usually offer a set of seminars where a lecturer or tutor would explain how a student could have gone about answering a particular task. In such a case, it is expected you would review your own work in light of your individual feedback on your coursework and group feedback given in a group seminar.

Remember, the fees currently payable per annum to attend university can seem quite daunting. Thus, looking at your studies purely from an economic perspective, and thus as a financial investment in yourself, it makes sense that you should want to pass, and pass well at that! Alternatively, and perhaps more desirably, by deciding to study for a degree, you are expressing a desire to learn more about a specific subject area simply for a personal love of the subject. Previously, you may have felt compelled to study A Levels or GCSEs. Now, however, it really is your choice and thus, entirely your responsibility. If you want to pass, work hard, aim high and who knows, you may surprise yourself.

Understanding Grade Definitions

Before you begin your first year, you need to be aware of the grade definitions used at university. Unlike A Levels, and many other qualifications, you do not attain a final A-C grade. Instead, you will attain a First, Second or Third Class degree certificate. These do not equate, strictly speaking, to an A B C as you would conventionally understand them. For example, the Second Class degree certificate, in most cases, is broken down further into a 2:1 or a 2:2. Also, in several universities, a First can be offered with special distinction or other additions, to recognise special achievement if significantly higher than expectations. Broadly speaking, the grade boundaries for undergraduate students are as follows:

1st	70%+
2:1	60%+ most jobs that specify a specific degree as a requisite require a 2:1 or above, as do most universities for those students wishing to pursue a Masters Degree.
2:2	50%+ most jobs that require a general degree usually ask for a 2:2 or above.
3rd	45%+
Pass	40%+

Please take note of the percentage regarding the highest qualification, a First, which if attained would certainly show an excellent grasp of the subject and guarantee a promising future. Some of my students, understandably, have been surprised by this and ask, "Doesn't this seem a bit low?" The short answer is yes. However, this is because, interestingly, in many subjects within higher education students seldom attain higher than 80%. To do so, I was once told by a lecturer, you would need to create a new and plausible theory. If we reflect on the reason for this, it is because a question within the humanities (philosophy etc.) rarely has a single correct answer, and this is subsequently reflected in the marking criteria. After all, you cannot attain 100% where there is no conclusive agreement. Having said that, there is agreement in respect of the conventions regarding what makes a good essay and argument. This is what you must learn to replicate when studying a written subject.

I am always reluctant to mention the words 'new theory' in front of undergraduate students. Inevitably there are those who attempt to create something *new*, albeit badly. Thus, I advise most of my students to avoid the urge to create something new, especially in the first year. On the other hand, if you feel compelled to try something experimental, the first year is certainly a better place to do so as your final degree classification is less likely to suffer as a result if something goes wrong.

Whatever you choose to do, you should always approach a written task with humility; it is likely that there will have been hundreds of thousands of essays written on the same subject before yours, and there will be many more written throughout your life. Remember, by the end of the first year of study, you want to have learnt how to produce 2:1 or 1st class essays consistently and replicate this in your second and third years.

Importantly, keep in mind that many universities apply progressively tougher marking criteria as you progress through your years of study; this means that the quality of submitted essays is expected to improve year on year; your essays will be marked stringently in the second and third years, whereas, in the first year, more allowances will be made. As a result, for example, it is possible to attain higher marks towards the end of your first year of study in comparison with the beginning of the second year of study. This dip in attainment is common and quickly rectifies as you continue to improve.

Marking Criteria

A Third Class degree is usually the lowest degree classification you can be awarded by a university. The future value of such an achievement will be limited, unless attained from a top university; even then, it is not ideal. The majority of students do not attain this classification and so while those who attain a Third join the ranks of the *officially* well educated, they are at the lower end of the spectrum. Some universities distinguish between a Pass (40 – 45%) and a Third Class degree (46 – 49%).

If you attain a Third Class degree classification, your essays will generally show you have a basic grasp of the subject at the higher education level. You are aware of the main principles related to your field and are able to show a working knowledge of them. However, essays of this class usually tend to list important points within a subject area instead of demonstrating any in-depth analysis. There may be errors in relation to accuracy of application and key theorists in the related field omitted. Evaluation is limited and basic.

What to know about Second Class degree/essays (Lower Division - 2:2)

It has been said, those who attained a 2:2 didn't drink enough to get a Third or study enough to get a 2:1; a mediocre classification which is neither bad nor particularly good. In the main, you will not be able to study further with this classification, as most universities expect a higher grade from Masters Degree applicants (a Masters is the next level of study which can be taken after a degree and generally represents the forefront of the discipline). However, it is not unheard of for students who attain a 2:2, if on the higher end of this boundary, to be accepted into a Masters course, under special consideration.

If you attain a 2:2 degree classification, your essays will generally show you have an acceptable knowledge of the subject at higher education level. Students within this classification usually demonstrate the ability to create self-contained arguments, which are supported with evidence. Essays of this class, while not going into considerable depth, show an awareness of relevant theorists and an understanding of their theories. A key clause found within this classification is: any arguments are, in the main, self-contained and therefore do not flow naturally within essays.

What to know about Second Class degree/essays (Higher Division - 2:1)

Attaining a 2:1 degree would show you have a good understanding of the subject, as expected at university, and prove that you are able to navigate fluently though the material. Those who attain a 2:1 stand a good chance of using the degree to attain relevant employment in the near future. Also, by attaining this classification, the possibility of future study remains securely open.

If you attain a 2:1 degree classification, your essays will generally show a good knowledge of the theorists in the field, evaluation of them and the ability to create a sustained argument in your essays. The latter is paramount. The fundamental difference between a 2:2 and a 2:1 in many marking criteria is the higher classification shows evidence of linking theorists' ideas and evaluating them accumulatively to create a sustained logical argument and conclusion. Those students who attain a 2:1 degree show an understanding of essential features regarding questions within the discipline and are able to demonstrate a clear focus on those issues.

What to know about the 1st Class degree/essays

The illusive First. This is your target. In my experience, the number of students who attain this qualification number approximately 10%. I was once told by a colleague that to attain a First, the student must send a chill down the neck of the reader. How exactly this is done is somewhat subjective, but I admire the echo of truth within her statement. I would describe this as understanding the cutting edge of the discipline and being able to debate within this sphere. More objectively, this could be described as being self critical of your own argument and acknowledging your presuppositions, while at the same time completing all the requirements for the 2:1 classification.

If you attain a First Class degree, you will have shown the required skills have been met in full. The possibility of future study remains open. Occasionally, students who attain a first omit a Masters and go straight for the PhD (the pinnacle of education) after some employment experience, or MPhil (a sort of half PhD, similar to a Masters, but more writing intensive – sometimes with exams/coursework elements). Employers actively seek out undergraduates of this calibre. Your essays will generally demonstrate knowledge at the forefront of the discipline. You will be able to create a sustained argument and evaluate theorist convincingly. In addition, you will also be self-critical of your evaluations and wholly aware of any assumptions or implications thereof.

Remember

Whatever you achieve, if you can look back at the end of three years (or up to 6 years if you are on a part time course) and say "I tried my best", then you should be proud of who you are and what you have achieved. Having a degree certificate, in one sense, simply gives you a bit of additional paper, but in another, it is a jewel in the crown of a completed education.

Writing Introductions – the basics

You will no doubt have heard about a host of different writing styles from various educators which at times even contradict one-another. This is not because those teaching you cannot agree about essay requirements, but because there is seldom one correct way of writing; if your writing is grammatical and lucid, it *is* correct. The beauty of literature is found in its fluidic nature; like music art and drama, there is not a correct way, but simply a way. Having said that, there are some generic expectations to be found in introductions and understanding these conventions will enable you to show a clear structure in your essay from the beginning. (I include a checklist on p.19 which lists these conventions).

Marks are available for demonstrating good structure in an essay. This will show that your thoughts are ordered and that you have spent some time thinking about how to approach the question. Thus, do take a moment before writing your essay to consider exactly what you have been asked to do and carry out the appropriate research necessary. A marker can usually tell whether an essay is following a clear structure, or not, from the introduction. You should see your introduction as a first opportunity to impress your examiners with your knowledge of the subject and deploy material directly relevant to the set question, in order to present the *spectrum of thought.*

When writing your introductions, avoid (like the plague) an introduction that waffles on for 500 words when your word count is only 2000 words. Likewise, when your lecturers tell you: "Keep the intro short", they never mean simply one sentence. As a general rule, the length of an introduction should be approximately 10% of the total word count, and no more. An effective introduction should include different elements depending on the purpose of the essay, but all attempts should be lucid, concise and as close as possible to the 10% limit. So, if your total word count is 2000, the introduction should be no more than 200 words. From the introduction, the reader should be able to ascertain exactly what the essay will be addressing and understand your position. Note, this does not necessarily mean that it should include your conclusion.

It has been noted by some study skill tutors that it is advisable not to give away your whole position in the introduction. This is true to an extent. On the one hand, you want the reader to be clear regarding your position from the outset and the introduction is paramount to this aim. However, on the other hand, you also want to show development throughout your essay. Something that can often confuse young writers is the need to balance these two imperatives. Thus, remember, it is not the purpose of an introduction to formulate a holistic argument; the main thrust of the essay: the main propositions, evaluations and so on, are usually expected to be developed throughout the essay and stated, in a humble manner, in the conclusion. However, it is important to demonstrate a clear understanding of the discipline and an awareness of where your view will sit on the *spectrum of thought* within the discipline. To do this, you will need to analyse the key elements of the question as early as possible.

Writing Introductions
– a little more

When writing your introduction, it is important to be aware that every academic work is conditioned by the context of contemporary academia. Nothing is written in a vacuum and every author is, in some way, representing a particular view, even if the work appears to be unbiased. When writing an introduction for a particular topic, it is imperative that you understand the *nerve of the question*. That is to say, how and where does it fit in the wider context? By understanding this, you will be in a position to write an effective introduction and essay.

As a general guide, these are points you can cover mentally before beginning. They will help in the formation of your ideas and creation of your essay plan, and also help you demonstrate the conventions that are typically expected.

Introduction Check List

A book review should show/mention/comment on:

• An awareness of the author; a short explanation of his/her position in his/her field of study would be advantageous.

- The article itself; is it adopting a critical or supportive approach to the respective question/topic? I.e. what is the context of the text?

- Is the article/book representing a typical position for the author, or does it represent a newly informed view? If so, what is different/the same? Make links with other works, if relevant.

- Where does the author's view sit on the *spectrum of thought* within the topic; i.e. who else has commented on the topic, how is the author's position the same/different from others within the discipline.

- Is the author approaching the topic from a sceptical or a supportive position?

An essay on a theological/philosophical question should show an awareness of:

- What is the essence of the question? This can be hard to grasp at first; start with your reading list and lecture notes.

- Are there any implications of the aforementioned essence? Most likely, there will be multiple implications and understanding these will help you become aware of the range of interpretations within the topic.

- What, if anything, is/was the author trying to avoid?

Note:

Seldom do theological or philosophical questions stand alone, e.g. what is asserted in Christology will affect what can be said in Mariology. Likewise, what is asserted in epistemology will affect what can be said in hermeneutics, etc. Many sub-categories within the respective disciplines are bound together in a manner which can be misunderstood (or wholly missed) by undergraduate students. Thus, background reading is essential; your *Reading List* is an essential starting point. This will be provided at the beginning of each module by your lecturers.

It is important to understand how a particular area of study fits into the wider discipline, as it will help orientate you regarding the *spectrum of thought* surrounding the set question. You may want to ask your lecturer/tutor directly "What is the spectrum of thought on this topic" during a tutorial or in the lecture hall. That is, what are the extremities of view on x, and the academic consensus on x?

- Who is/are the key thinker/s in the respective field and what is his/her position?
- How is/are the key point/s similar or different from another theorist's position within the topic?

- What are the philosophical/theological implications of the question?

An evaluation of poetry or other literature:

- Who is the writer and when was it written? Ask yourself, what was happening in society at the time and consider the personal context in relation to wider context.
- How does the poem/literature address a particular human reality - if at all?
- Speculate (briefly) on why the poem/text was written.
- Commentators/other poet's/writer's view of the poem/ literature.

An essay (in general) should:

- Present your position for which you will argue in a fair manner.
- Show awareness of *relevant* theorists who hold alternative views, be they contemporary or of old.
- Show an awareness of the spectrum of thought and present your position on this spectrum.

The above points can be used interchangeably between different disciplines; choose those which best suit your exact title.

The Introduction Checklist above gives you a basic formula which can be used to improve your introductions. However, there is more. As aforementioned, there is a different grading system used to that at A Level. It is important to realise that evidence of each of these levels might be found throughout an essay, which naturally includes the introduction. Thus, the more you know about a particular topic, the more effective will be your introduction in presenting the key arguments and, ultimately, their evaluation throughout the essay which will support your conclusion. In metaethics, for example, to understand A.J Ayer's Emotivism, you must also understand G.E Moore's Intuitionism. This is because the two theories are, one could argue, essentially opposites. You will introduce key concepts for your questions better if you have some knowledge of its opposite because, by knowing the context, you will be able to do so in the manner that it was intended.

Please note: this is not to say, "Write an essay on the opposite!" I once marked an essay which was supposed to present the strengths and weaknesses of deontological ethics. Instead, I received an excellent exposition of teleological theorists and their ideas. Sadly, if you do not answer the question, you cannot receive marks; this is analogous to hiring a builder to construct a conservatory, and instead finding a new toilet in the kitchen. Perhaps useful, but certainly unexpected and not something you would pay for. Examiners can become disgruntled when faced with clearly intelligent responses albeit to a question which was never asked!

A good tip is to avoid the above by having three highlighters - yellow, red and green (or whatever colours you like). Highlight those restrictive words or clauses in red, directions in yellow and key words (topical) in green.

Example

Describe Anselm's ontological argument as it is found in Proslogion chapters 2 & 3 and compare this with a later form of the argument.

By doing this, you would dissect the question into:

Green	What you should specifically focus on: 'Anselm's Ontological Argument'.
Red	Your restrictions (so basically, focus on the green part in light of the red part). Here, you would only look at Anselm's ontological argument as it is presented in 'Proslogion chapters 2 & 3' and also 'a later form of the argument'.
Yellow	'Describe' & 'compare'.

Additional comments:

The question example above gives you a very good indication regarding concepts surrounding the development of Anselm's ontological argument. This is because there are two restrictive clauses: 'Proslogion chapter 2 & 3', and 'a later form of the argument'; so clearly Anselm's ontological argument has at least two expressions. After understanding this, to write a good essay you would now focus on the 'yellow part': describe the differences and compare (including strengths and weaknesses) the two formulations.

It is imperative you read a broad range of material on your module topics. I remind you, once again, of your reading list which will be set by your lecturers at the beginning of each module. Once you have orientated yourself in the subject material, remember to stay focused when writing and always ask yourself at the end of each paragraph; is this answering the question? A method that you can use to effectively ensure that you are on task is to follow the '6 point method', which can be found on p.58.

Introduction Example

Here is an example of a weak introduction for a book review written for an ethics module at university:

Ethics

Question: *Evaluate Peter Singer's article Famine Affluence and Morality*

> *To Evaluate Peter Singer's article famine affluence and morality we must first distinguish the key points that singer raised in his article. He begins with the admitted assumption that suffering and death from lack of food, shelter, and medical care are bad. I agree with this assumption, I will give however unlike Singer a reason for my assumption. This is because I believe this to be intrinsically wrong. Singer's manor of putting this point forwards perhaps implies this, however I do not agree with the way that he does this as he simply does not state it.*

Here, the student has demonstrated evidence of reading, at least part of *Peter Singer's article Famine Affluence and Morality*. This is shown where the student introduces a premise within the article: suffering that comes from a lack of food, shelter etc. is bad. However, the student then criticises Singer's article (I think unfairly) while adding nothing. The student has not shown any awareness of the context of Singer's article or its position in the wider discussion. All we know after reading this introduction is that 'Peter Singer assumes suffering is bad'; the student agrees with this because it is intrinsically wrong; the student thought Singer did not offer sufficient reason for this premise.

Compare now the differences between the previous and this student's introduction for the same question:

Famine Affluence and Morality was written in 1972 by Peter Singer in response to a natural disaster that devastated Bengal. Singer's aim was to argue nations objectively into action following what he felt was an apparent apathy in the face of suffering. Singer's utilitarian approach sparked a debate among other ethicists, such as G Hardin and J Arthur, which continues in various forms to the present day. Singer's key theory, of giving to the point of Marginal Utility, is based upon a set of premises; the first of which being an assumption, that 'suffering and death from lack of food, shelter and medical care is bad'. Once this premise is accepted, a logical argument follows which compels richer individuals to give to poorer ones.

It is not surprising the first of these two essays went on to scrape a 3rd, the second essay a 1st. If we analyse the key differences found in the introduction we can begin to understand why.

(**Task:** before reading the table below, try and highlight the first of the two introductions to find all mistakes, both grammatical and logical. Have you found any oddities?)

Weaker Essay (3rd)	**Stronger Essay (1st)**
We do not know why the article was written.	The context of the article is given.
No evidence of awareness regarding the *spectrum of thought on* the topic.	While their positions are not outlined, an awareness of G. Hardin and J. Arthur is shown in the introduction. – It would have been better if the student, briefly, mentioned these views.
Summary of article not given.	Summery of article evident.

Grammatical errors and incorrect words used. Also evidence of odd phraseology. For example: manor instead of manner. 'Admitted assumption'.	A better use of English evident.
The first premise of the argument is given alone and then unfairly criticised; in any written discipline, an opinion must not simply be stated, it must be logically arrived at.	The first premise is given as well as key vocabulary associated with the article. The implication of the first premise is presented.

How's your English; Building Block

It is imperative your command of the English language is sufficient to meet the needs of your studies. For international students wishing to study at university this means:

IELTS	Level 6.5 – 7	International English language testing system

TOEFL	93 – 100	Test of English as a foreign language
CEFR	C1	Common European framework reference
GCSE*	C or above	General certificate of secondary education

acceptable in some universities following a written application.

It is very tempting for home grown students to assume their grasp of the English language, particularly written English, is perfect. This is rarely the case, especially if you are someone who has had little experience of writing essays before university. This is because we are implicitly very much bidialectic (if not tri-dialectic) i.e. fluent in several spoken dialects. We use these interchangeably, depending on the social context in which we find ourselves. Essay writing, while it certainly possesses an element of the author's writing style, does not follow the same conventions as spoken dialects; sometimes, this can be difficult to distinguish: the way you write is not necessarily the same as the way you speak.

Therefore, all students should set aside additional time to write a first draft, which can then be re-edited. Always read through your work, even if you feel confident when writing essays. (Word's spell check will usually miss incorrect words. For example, common mistakes include: *there* and *their, practise and practice, whole and hole etc.*)

When redrafting your work, if you have read something many times you may add, omit or even change words as you read. This can happen when spending long periods of time in front of a computer screen. The best way to avoid common mistakes is to print your essay and put it to one side. Then, get it out several days before the due date and read it afresh. By doing this, when you return to re-edit your work shortly before handing it in, you will be more likely to notice any errors and be able to correct them.

A second suggestion, only relevant if you are proof-reading specifically for spelling errors, is to read your text in reverse: start at the end and read sentences backwards until you reach the start of your essay. This can be a little frustrating, as your reading speed will decrease because you are reading 'in the wrong direction'. However, you are more likely to pick up spelling mistakes in the process.

There are short courses available that will specifically aid in the development of your academic writing skills. Enquire with your university for details of these. In some cases subsidies are available. In others, free short courses are offered in-house (i.e. by the university) to help improve the academic writing skills of students. If this is not available, I suggest googling 'Open University short courses'; the OU provides many free short study skill and writing courses. You can enrol on a course after an initial account has been created.

I now provide you, as a brief guide, a 'building block' which can be used to create an introduction. Consider creating several of your own which can be adapted to your subject needs.

INTRODUCTION EXAMPLES AND A BUILDING BLOCK

Building block   Statement
                        Implication
                        Evidence
                        How/Why others can use the statement
                        Goal

Please see this building block as a structure for an introductory paragraph. Use it in conjunction with the introduction checklist in the previous section. Remember, adapt this as appropriate to best suit your set question. I have used two examples to demonstrate how this can be moulded to your respective needs.

Theology

Question: *Franz Rosenzweig view of interreligious dialogue*

Interreligious dialogue is fraught with difficulties; the more two faiths agree, it can be argued, the more diluted they become. *(statement)*

Thus, for a faith that maintains a claim of absolute truth, dialogue with others from different faiths can shake the foundations of orthodox belief. *(implication)*

In the 20th & 21st centuries, we have witnessed a form of extremism that can come from a fear of dialogue and due respect for *the other*, e.g. The Shoah and Terrorism. *(evidence)*

In recent decades inter-religious documents, for example the Dabru Emet, have been used by theologians, irrespective of faith, to build bridges between different groups and work together for human unity and the common good; qualities that were in short supply during the previous century that saw two world wars, genocides and other atrocities unmatched in human history. *(how/why others can use the statement)*

Franz Rosenzweig, an early 20th Century Jewish theologian, engaged in such dialogue with Eugen Rosenstock-Huessy, his Christian lecturer at Leipzig University, long before the Shoah. It is possible such inter-religious dialogue can provide an answer to future tragedies. *(goal)*

Please note the first statement does not have to be a supporting statement of the author's position. We see in this introduction that the opening statement in fact highlights a possible problem for interreligious dialogue as opposed to its merits. Rosenzweig is only introduced at the end as a *goal* because he offered a tolerant (and certainly unique) view of Jewish-Christian relations. His views can later be argued as a solution to intolerance or logically dismissed.

EXAMPLE OF BUILDING BLOCK ADAPTED.

Statement

Implication

Evidence

How the author criticises the argument

Philosophy of Religion

Question: *How did Kant criticise the Ontological Argument?*

All ontological arguments, found mainly in Christian theology, aim to argue, using analytics, that existence is a predicate of God. *(statement)*

The main criticism of ontological arguments is that they can create an illogical jump between rational statements and empirical knowledge. It is here that Kant's criticism is most clearly understood. *(implication)*

While it can be said Kant's argument primarily rebuts Descartes formulation of the ontological argument, Kant also highlights problems for all such arguments. In the Critique of Pure Reason, Kant expounded his concept of a priori and a posteriori knowledge, i.e. that which is known innately and that which is known through experience. For Kant, existence cannot be a predicate in and of itself regarding an a priori statement. *(how the author criticises the argument)*.

INTRODUCTIONS - TIPS AND ACTIVITIES

You need to practise writing introductions for a host of questions. Therefore, find a friend or ask your classmates to make pairs and each of you try writing an introduction, of no more than 250 words on any topic of your choosing. Then, swap this paragraph with a friend/classmate, without divulging the title. See if you can guess your classmate's titles and make a plan on what would be the content of the essay using information from the introduction only.

Task: Below you will find some essay introductions written by students in 1st, 2nd or 3rd year. After reading an introduction, try to formulate a question that would merit a student to write such an introduction. Can you see an outline or essay structure emerging?

(Within Theology – 216 words)

*Elie Wiesel, a survivor of Auschwitz and then Buchenwald,
endured beatings, hunger, roll calls and other tortures. He was
one of millions sent to concentration camps across Nazi held
Europe, who, owing to the 2nd World War, lost his faith in a
personal benevolent God. He believed, 'You will sooner or later
be confronted with the enigma of God's action in history'. From
this, a key question arises when addressing Jewish responses to
the Holocaust. It is not a question of how humanity is capable
of such atrocities; Stanley Milgram showed how this is possible,
instead, it is found in Philosophy of Religion. In this light, how can
Judaism maintain its traditional faith following Shoah; a terrible
event that caused suffering and damage, both physically and
theologically. Different Jewish theologians have attempted to
provide an answer to this question. Emiel Fackenheim introduced
a 614th commandment, 'Thou shall survive'; significant for Jews
because traditionally there are 613 commandments in the Jewish
Scriptures. Ignaz Maybaum introduced the idea of the Holocaust
being a third Churban (catastrophe); significant because the
previous two were tied closely to Jewish history. Most radically,
Elchonon Wasserman believed God's wrath came upon his
people because of their lack of Torah observance. In this essay,
I will focus on the response given by Maybaum.*

(Within Ethics – 227 words)

The Euthyphro dilemma is found in Plato's dialogue Euthyphro. Socrates, Plato's teacher, asks Euthyphro, "Is the pious loved by the gods because it is pious, or is it pious because it is love by the gods". The subtle difference in the order of Socrates' question outlines a continuing and fundamental investigation found within meta-ethics. That being, how do we define terms like good, right and wrong? Does goodness exist objectively, or is it instead subjective? What is good? Meta ethics, unlike normative-ethics, is not concerned with actions but with the reasons, meaning and the identification, if at all possible, of ethical meaning.

Many meta-ethicists have attempted to conclusively answer the Euthyphro dilemma and assert whether ethical statements can have meaning. A.J Ayer, a member of the Vienna Circle, introduced Emotivism as a response to G.E Moore's Intuitionism; arguing that as ethical statements are neither analytical nor synthetic, they are, thus, meaningless and nothing more than expressions of emotion. However, Ross supported, as did Prichard, Moore's position and instead added 7 key Prima Facé duties in an attempt to account for different ethical assertions. The array of different ethical stances, I believe, is best understood by Prichard's introduction of reason within Intuitionism. Likewise, it is with a level of reasoning that Ross distinguishes between his 7 Prima Facé duties. In this essay, I will focus on Moore's theory.

(Within Philosophy of Religion – 120 words)

An ontological argument can be used to prove the existence of God in an analytical manner. To do so, an analytical approach would be adopted and little reference made to empirical observations. However, for many atheists, such as Dawkins, this approach remains insufficient. This is because the approach is not based on empirical data. Thus, as there is no connection with empirical data, for a realist, any such theory is irrelevant as it is purely based upon 'word games'. Also, it is the case that an ontological argument, while it can be used in a religious manner, as is done by Anslem, can also be used to disprove the existence of God, as Dawkins shows us in the God Delusion.

(Within Ethics – 174 words)

It can be argued that Virtue Ethics is both objective and subjective. The theory is primarily concerned with the development of society by the way of bettering the individual; Aristotle believed a person, by finding the Golden Mean between extreme behaviours, can learn to be virtuous. This theory is often contrasted to traditional normative theories such as deontology, which emphasises objective duties and teleology, which discerns right from wrong by the outcome of an action and is therefore subject to the outcome.

Thus, it is not immediately clear which of these categories, objective or subjective, the verification theory falls under. As, there is an exemplary behaviour which is to be adhered to: the Golden Mean. This can be understood in an objective manner when looking at the overall rule, i.e 'be virtuous', 'do the Golden Mean' etc. However, the Golden Mean itself, by which we discern how to be virtuous, is bound by the understanding of society or the individual as the extremities are deemed by society, and thus, in this respect, is subjective.

(Church History – 326 words)

The Council of Chalcedon, which commenced on the 8th October and concluded on the 1st November 451, is seen as the 4th ecumenical council by the Eastern Orthodox & Roman Catholic Churches. Official contemporary figures indicate five-hundred and twenty bishops were in attendance during the four week period of discussions, though this is not conclusive as the preserved acts for individual sessions seldom records more than 300 present at any one time. Set in Bithynia Asia Minor, modern day Turkey, the council is upheld as one of the triumphs of orthodoxy by most churches. Its legacy has survived to date through The Church primarily in what is known as the Chalcedonian Definition.

The Council of Chalcedon was primarily convened to offer a treatment of christology that represented the orthodox view to which all could agree. As we see, shortly before, unorthodox christologies were pushed forward by their advocators Eutychus and Nestorius. Though The Church understood these christologies to be incorrect, due to the repercussions they had either upon the Theotokos or soteriology, there was no single answer readily available with which to respond to these individuals. Patriarch

Anatolius of Constantinople, and others, pushed for the Council of Chalcedon to provide such an answer. By doing this the Council set to address previous failings found in the Second Council of Ephesus, which came to be known as The Robber Council. I mention this because the Council of Chalcedon cannot be understood in isolation; many would argue it is especially linked to Ephesus II in respect to the backlash towards it.

In this essay I shall attempt to assess the achievement of Chalcedon. I shall do this by first looking at the contemporary heresies of the time and then ask how the christology of Chalcedon avoids these failings. Following this, I shall examine how the role of language affected the overall achievement of the council in regards to the two theological schools of thought prominent at the time.

(Answers are found at the end of the book).

The middle part – continuing a good start

When trying to understand how to write a good essay, I believe it is imperative to be aware of Benjamin Bloom's taxonomy (I include the revised version below). It is an extremely useful guide which students can use to understand the developmental process of an essay. Likewise, if you compare the pyramid to any marking criteria you will find correlations between top marks and the top end of Bloom's taxonomy.

Bloom led a group of educational psychologists in the 1950s; they developed a classification of levels of intellectual behaviour important in learning. I believe these skills, if you will, can be learnt and applied to essay writing techniques. If done correctly, it will enhance your writing style and improve your discernment in regard to what should be included in an essay and when it becomes relevant.

Last   Creating

                    Evaluating

                    Analysing

                    Applying

                    Understanding

First   Remembering

Bloom's Taxonomy

- Remembering
- Understanding
- Applying

Every student, in order to write a good essay, must remember the basic facts which are relevant to the set question. In the original taxonomy this was not *remembering* but *knowledge* and is, perhaps, more easily understood when referring to teaching methods. In addition, all students must at least understand the subject matter and be able to apply it effectively in its natural intention. Howsoever you remember these, when writing the middle sections of your essay, you must be clear on these points:

Remembering

'To remember facts' is the first learning outcome for all students and, as Bloom's taxonomy indicates, the foundation of higher skills. As children, we remember the alphabet, how to count etc. and as we grow, the names of key thinkers, their theories and important dates. The better you become at the early stages of the taxonomy, the more you will be able to gain marks for breadth of knowledge.

It is important that information you present in your essay is directly relevant to the question. There will no doubt be a reading list which you can access. This will encompass the core knowledge of your respective subjects. Part of your marks will be allocated to how well you have remembered what you have been taught, and also to how well you have selected relevant knowledge from what you have learnt from both the reading list and independent research.

Understanding

Without this second stage, remembering facts would be nothing more than regurgitation; this will limit your marks and does not suffice at university; without demonstrating that you understand the facts, you will be limited to a 3rd classification, if you're lucky. Thus, you must, in the course of your essay writing development, show understanding of what you know. The way this is done will vary from the set question to the writing styles, but a key feature of this approach is that understanding is done accurately. Do not attempt to put words into a theorist's mouth that were never there or 'create a manikin' to knock down. While you may be aware of the first advice, the latter may be unfamiliar to you as in A Levels, for example, students were primarily accustomed to simply memorising points of view for a said argument and using 'however/on the other hand/whereas' etc., to create a weak response which would allow students to continue their main argument (one of memory, in the main) without real hindrance.

At this level, to simply create a weak argument to knock down is unhelpful to your marks. This is because to do so you would not be representing the argument fairly in all likelihood; therefore, you would be at a disadvantage and lose marks for not presenting the argument accurately (i.e. in context etc.). For this reason, it is better to create an argument which represents a theorist fairly – which cannot be dismissed easily, rather than an argument which can be dismissed easily that does not represent the true opinion of the said theorist.

Did you know?

On Google Books you can type a quote and the search engine will search through millions of books and find those books which contain the exact wording of your search. This can be a very useful tool when trying to find supporting/opposing quotes for a point of view; I recommend this resource to my students in addition to, and *not* instead of, reading lists. For example, if you wanted to find a book, simply type in the title and you will find the book and all other books which make reference to your search; alternatively, you can search for a quote you wish to find, and books containing the *exact* wording will be displayed with page numbers including the searched wording.

However, use this feature with caution; a student once wrote an essay and attempted to use this feature without reading the chapter, (if only he had read the paragraph he would have realised his mistake). The student had searched 'profuse belief in God' and then quoted Richard Dawkins professing a 'profuse belief in God', the irony. On the contrary, the author had written a sentence and stipulated the view as nonsensical. Thus, if you use choose to use this technique, always read the surrounding section before you quote anything or you could end up a little embarrassed.

Thus, understanding an argument accurately will allow you to conduct additional research and make use of materials that are not necessarily on your reading list. This is because by accurately understanding a point of view, you will be able to select relevant materials to use in your essay. It is advisable to use books from your reading list in the first instance, and also to include several that you have deemed appropriate yourself as this will show that you have undertaken independent research into the subject area which, if done well, will impress your examiners and improve your grade.

Remember when reading, especially primary texts, to be aware of *hermeneutics*. This is the study of *text interpretation* (chiefly to do with scripture, however it is applicable to all areas of study).

When you read something you are bound by your own *academic baggage*. Clearly, your personal experience and previous education will directly impact on your interpretation of anything you hear, see and read.

Exercise to understand hermeneutics:
Read this poem out aloud and record yourself on your mobile phone (or dictaphone if you have one) as you read it for the first time.

My Journey
gives you Answers

give you Truth

opens your eyes to Problems

earn you Sympathy

due to Pain

with a Tear

of the Heart

gains Courage

is being Brave

to admit Defeat

makes you Ask

why...

Once you have done so, ask yourself these questions: do you understand the poem? If so, what do you think the author is trying to say? Do you think there is a philosophy evident in the poem? Then, read it silently several times, after your first reading/recording, considering these questions.

Now, simply replay the poem using your device and follow the text as you listen to the recording you made. Consider: have you missed or added any words? Why in such a way? How did you say the last word of the 6th line? Why like that? Where did you stop? Where did you start? Why so?

Finally, read the poem aloud again, including the title, and repeat every word that is capitalised in the body of the poem. Has your understanding or reading of the poem changed and if so, how? Answer the above questions before reading the next section.

Note:

When I present this exercise to my students, I seldom tell them that I am the author of the poem; I find students are more confident in their analysis this way. Students are invited to answer the questions aforementioned, and I am always interested in the various interpretations and readings of the poem as they nearly always represent the student's history/

way of thinking, instead of that of the author; perhaps, the purpose of poetry is a mirror to one's soul.

> I wrote this poem when I was 13/14 years of age, and certainly had no knowledge of Friedrich Nietzsche. However, a student once gave me the most elaborate exposition which included Nietzsche's theory of eternal reoccurrence. Perhaps, simply because the question 'is there a philosophy evident' is asked, merits its search, but not its existence. This is very important to remember when writing any essay.

Always consider your personal baggage, that is to say your interpretation, and do not allow it to adversely affect your understanding of the author's intended meaning.

The 9 Dot Problem

Marcel Danesi, a professor of semiotics and anthropology at Victoria College, University of Toronto, was able to trace 'the 9 dot puzzle' back to 1914; found in the first edition of Sam Loyd's (1841 – 1911) *Encyclopaedia of Puzzles*. It is unclear where Loyd obtained (perhaps he created) this puzzle. I use it here to highlight the same theme as above. Specifically: consider your academic baggage.

In the 1960s, Walter Pauk, a true pioneer of study skills, presented this puzzle in his book '*How to Study in College*' so that it would open the mind of students to the complexities of studying within higher education. It covers a similar principle as the poetry analysis above. If you have not encountered it before, give it a go and consider the implications for studying at university.

Task:

With a pencil, try and connect the dots using only four straight lines and without taking your pencil off the page. Once you have passed through a dot, you cannot reuse that dot as a point of travel. (It is harder than you might think, but it is possible!).

(The answer is at the end of the book).

Applying

Applying in an essay is to put what you know into appropriate service; you need to show that you understand the theory's natural intended purpose and make direct references to that purpose. To apply correctly would be to represent a point of view in a way that was intended (see *understanding* previously), that is either in opposition or in support of a view. This is one way to obtain marks within application, though there is a second way. I wrote previously that you must not put words into an author's mouth. I still maintain this, however, when it comes to application of theories, you can present an argument which asks, if the theory were applied in a different manner, what would be the outcome? However, do this with caution.

A second thing to be aware of regarding application is to understand the theory's natural intended application, i.e. the antithesis. While you may explore the possibilities of applying the theory in different ways, there is also the author's original intended application. In turn, students can slowly understand the Hegelian process. This will influence and enrich the understanding of the discipline. These are found, usually, in what many see as opposites within the *spectrum of thought*. Remember, even academics are bound by their previous revelations within hermeneutics:

For example:

Theism	Vs	Atheism
Empiricism	Vs	Rationalism
Teleological	Vs	Deontological
Emotiveism	Vs	Intuitionism
Monophysite	Vs	Dyophysite
Realism	Vs	Antirealism
Monists	Vs	Dualists
Irenaean Theodicy	Vs	Augustinian Theodicy

This list is by no means comprehensive and could go on almost indefinitely. Furthermore, I believe, it continually evolves in light of the ever developing, changing and retrospective light found within any discipline. The reason I include it here is to show you that every theory is in opposition to something. Find out what it is! The apophatic way (via negativa) shows us it is possible to distinguish things by their opposites. (It's opposite is cataphatic language).

'THE HIGHER ORDERS'

- Analysing
- Evaluating
- Creating

Analysing

Once you have applied the theory, you will be able to consider it in detail and subject the theory to analysis by way of highlighting essential features and/or meaning. Ask yourself a host of questions about the theory. Look in depth as to why the theorist has presented his/her findings in the way that she/he has. Consider the Hegelian process; how is it relevant here?

Evaluating

This is the greatest achievement of any essay. By evaluating successfully you will be able to access the full range of marks available in any marking criteria used at university. Beware of creating an essay that is wholly descriptive and does not demonstrate evaluation. Every student, from A Level upwards, must move away from simply the descriptive and towards evaluation. It means that you arrived at a critical position regarding the information presented, and have expounded whether it is convincing and said why is it so? The latter is of paramount importance regarding this stage of writing; without justifying your opinions with evidence, it becomes merely baseless meanderings.

Creating

I refer you to my comments at the beginning of this guide in respect to 'creating a new theory': no! Please wait until you are more versed in the subject before attempting something as bold as this. Keep in mind, there is no marking criteria, at this level, which requires you to create a new theory. Therefore, if you simply wish to attain good marks, follow the expected conventions and write essays that meet the standard you wish to attain. Do not think of the standard as the pass-mark borderline; if you fixate on this area alone, it will show a bad study habit developing.

On the other hand, I want my students to be original, creative and free thinking; question everything, even yourself, even me. Therefore, if you wish to write an experimental essay, by all means do so. But do not get too upset if you underachieve; sometimes, such approaches merit either a 1st or fail, and very little in between.

However, with age comes wisdom and, from my very limited wisdom, I can tell you that it is better to *tick the boxes* now and be creative later. After all, for all your creativity, your quirks and mannerisms, in the 'real world' (whatever that is), people may judge you, among other things, on your grades – like employers. Therefore, make them the best that you can.

Summary of Bloom's Taxonomy

You cannot create a credible essay unless you first demonstrate evaluation of existing academic sources. Likewise, you cannot evaluate unless you analyse, nor analyse unless you apply a theory, nor apply what you do not understand nor understand what you do know. Thus, Bloom's taxonomy correlates perfectly, not only to the order of learning, but also to the order of presentation in an essay. As ever, there are always exceptions in writing styles, for there is no single correct method, but observe an introduction seen previously, this time in the following sections:

- Remembering – Facts: dates / names / places
- Understanding – Implication / where x is situated on *the spectrum of thought* / why the fact / relevant background knowledge
- Applying – Give an example / illustrate
- Analyse – Compare & contrast / interpret / infer
- Evaluate – Provide the strengths and weaknesses / is it logical / judge / where are the 'chinks' in the armour / your position in light of the arguments (your voice)

Peter Singer wrote *Famine Affluence and Morality* in 1972, responding to a natural disaster that devastated the city of Bengal in India. *(Remembering/fact)*

Singer's aim was to objectively argue nations into action following, what he felt, an apathy that was apparent in the face of suffering. His extreme utilitarian approach sparked a debate among other ethicists, such as G Hardin and J Arthur; whereby the Notion of Entitlement and Marginal Utility were hotly debated. *(Understanding/why/background)*

Singer's argument is based upon a set of premises; the first of which being an assumption: that 'suffering and death from lack of food, shelter and medical care is bad'. Once this is accepted, a logical argument follows that compels richer individuals to give to poorer ones, until the point of Marginal Utility. *(Applying)*

If we compare the approaches of Hardin and Singer, one could say the first appears selfish and the other selfless – but is this a fair comparison? *(Analyse)*

In this essay I will argue that Singer's argument is both logical and valid, and can only be responded to by total immersion into charitable living. To do otherwise would be nothing short of hypocrisy. *(Evaluation/own voice)*

Conclusions – bringing it all together and the 6 point system

In the main, essay conclusions come in two formats: following either *The 10% Model* or *The Running Model*. Each has advantages and suits different students depending on their style of learning. Before I explain what these are, and which you should use depending on your writing style, please imagine the following scenario:

Consider

> You have been given an essay to write with a 2000 word limit and it is due in two weeks. You spend several days researching the topic, using materials provided and suggested by your lecturers. 12 days left now. Do you a) jump in and start writing or b) spend another day to create a plan?

Some students who answer a) do so because they feel as though there is not enough time and that if another whole day is spent not writing, they may not complete the essay on time. Or because they simply enjoy getting 'stuck in'. However, I would advise the b) approach. This is because a small amount of essay planning (which is different from essay research) enables you to divide every short essay (yes, 2000 words is a short essay) into 6 main points that logically follow on from each other and whose points are justified, using clear reasoning; every essay you produce will be coherent and convincing if you do this well. Furthermore, you will find that your write-up speed increases because, before you put pen to paper (or fingers to keyboards) you will have a clear idea of what you are going to do step by step.

The six point method sounds somewhat extravagant, but it is really quite simple: simply write 6 single sentences that are logical and follow on from each other.

For example:
6 Point Method Demonstrated

(Question within Theology)
Augustine on the City of God and the Earthly City

1. Augustine presents both the City of God and the Earthly City as distinguishable but interwoven mediums.
2. Each City can be broken down into two areas.
3. x could be interpreted as …   (use comparisons / secondary & primary sources)
4. y could be interpreted as …   (use comparisons / secondary & primary sources)

5. Those similarities are *v*, those distinguishing features are *z*. What could this suggest?

6. Therefore, Augustine may have meant *a, b, c* on *x* and *y* respectively.

If you allocate approximately 250 words to each of the points above, you will quickly develop a coherent essay. Add 10% (200) words for the introduction and again for the conclusion and you would have reached your word limit.

Conclusion; Running Model

In this model, it would be expected that you create sub-conclusions as you progress in the essay. This means that at the end of each planning section, there would be a conclusion summarising the argument thus far and postulating strengths/weakness (or simply a position) of the essay at the respective points.

Here, the final conclusion length would be shorter: tens of words instead of hundreds, so that you avoid tautology. Thus, the end of the essay (final conclusion) would be analogous to a summary of those sub-conclusions found previously and more focused on where your conclusion is situated on the *spectrum of thought* within the discipline.

Reasons to avoid this model:

- You are prone to deviation.
- You do not feel as though you fully understand the subject material.
- You do not usually write an essay in sequential order.

Each sub-conclusion must be focused. If it is not, there is a danger of confusing the overall direction of the essay. Then, the essay will appear confused and unclear. If you want to use this model, ensure that you write the introduction first and then each *part* (i.e. from the 6 point system) sequentially. Some people, for example, write conclusions before the main body of their essay; do not do this if you are using *The Running Model* as it is more likely to confuse than be of use using when taking this writing approach.

Conclusion; 10% model

In this format, your conclusion would be longer than the previous (a similar length as your introduction). You will largely follow Bloom's taxonomy for the main body of the essay and only after presenting all your arguments, which have been arrived at logically, would you present an extensive conclusion explaining the overall line of argumentation, your weakness/ assumptions and, most importantly, the repercussions. Be sure to include any presuppositions that lead you to the conclusion as this would be a 1st degree classification requirement.

Reasons to avoid this model:

- Your planning is weak or non-existent.
- You are writing your short essay over a longer period of time. Ideally, each essay should be planned. However, if it is not, it is better to use *the Running Model*. This is because *the 10% Model* only works if the information presented is very clear and relevant to the final conclusion. If it is not, there is the danger of omitting or adding information in the essay that would not suit the final conclusion in light of the main body of the essay; remember, it can take days to write an essay and minutes to read.

Perhaps you find that you share traits with regard to the reasons to avoid this model outlined above in both conclusion models. In such a case, experiment with both and see which you prefer. You may naturally lean towards *The Running Model* because, if you follow the 6 Point System, this may feel more natural. However, do try both and select the method which works best for you.

Study Skills - General

So far, I have presented you with expectations, hints and study skill tips specific to written subjects; looking at essay formulation as part of the main study focus. From this point onwards, I will address some of the more conventional study skills while trying to offer an interpretation of these specifically in light of written subjects.

Stronger students usually find this aspect of study skills a little rudimentary. However, I would advise giving it a chance as you might be surprised at how a structured approach to managing your time and note-making can have a really positive impact on your degree attainment. Likewise, knowing what type of learner you are can orientate you in your learning and also explain some of your past educational experiences; for example, a dyslexic individual who has been given a late diagnosis would usually find that they prefer visual learning instead of text-based learning. Or, for example, those who are more musical may prefer spoken input.

Note Making

Simple Methods

Note making is one of the study skill areas that is often, and sadly, neglected by students. This is because it is an area that may appear to be of little significance when studying within higher education, or anywhere else for that matter. However, for those studying written subjects at university, it is second only to essay writing and research. This is because it converts a primary learning medium (the lecture hall) into a format that can be accessed repetitively. Furthermore, all students who make and keep organised notes will be in a better situation when it comes to revision.

So how should one make notes? There are two main extensive methods which I will cover in the next section and several simpler methods; the simpler methods may feature within the extensive methods themselves. Please consider that all simpler methods require conversion into revision notes; it will not be as effective to simply read your class notes when revising. Those students revising in such a manner are likely to find that a lot of time is spent revising without significant results and in all honesty, this does not count as effective revision. However, for the extensive note making methods the same does not necessarily follow, as you will see.

Please read the following methods and choose the one that best suits your learning style.

The Solid Block Writing Method

This is perhaps the simplest note making method (if it can even be called a note making method) and has been described by many study skill tutors as quite ineffective. I myself, however, do find some merit in this system, but only if one can touch type, and if the student has access to a laptop during the lecture. This method is simply writing verbatim (word for word, or as close as possible) everything the lecturer says. Older study skill guides will usually tell you to avoid this approach altogether, however, this was before the computerised generation. I regularly meet young students who can type far faster than they can write by hand (I myself am one of them and certainly used this method successfully for a short time) but after realising its limitations I changed to another system. Namely, it is time consuming as the notes have to be revisited and by the end of a two hour lecture, you can quite easily have several thousand words to review.

If you use this method, you must ensure that you later read and edit your notes (as soon as possible, ideally on the same day) into a revisable format; for example: revision cards, short points to learn, into the Outline or Mapping Methods.

Otherwise, your effectiveness during revision will be drastically reduced; it is not easy to read and absorb a vast amount of text; Edgar Dale suggested (and proved) "We remember approximately 10% of what we read after two weeks". Thus, conversion into another format is essential.

The Outline Method

The Outline Method is when a student makes notes based on a running format of bullet points that are directly relevant to the previous. Each point should be indented further than the previous, in order to be easily distinguishable. After each thread of argumentation or theory, the student should start the thread again at the far left of the page.

For example:

P1

  P2 (which follows from P1)

New P1

  P2 (which follows from New P1)

    P3 (which follows from P2 above)

      P4 (ibid).

Here, you will create a series of arguments and/or 'lines of logic'. This is particularly useful if you are studying a subject like philosophy or theology because it allows you to see, at a glance, the overall theory, its premises and direction. However, you will need to edit your class notes into something more extensive while the information is fresh in your mind. Otherwise, you may risk omitting something substantial that is important to the clear understanding of the argument. It is advisable, where possible, to create a revision card for each individual line of argument (dependant on length) and present its strength and weakness.

The Mapping Method

The Mapping Method, or mind map, is a visual map that enables a quick overview of the subject material at a glance. However, depth is harder to capture without writing hefty amounts in a particular area, which could spoil the format, and would thus defeat the purpose of a mind map, which is: to create an easily understood visual presentation of information.

The Mapping Method is particularly good for those students who learn best using visual input; creating a mind map is the easiest application of this. It is also quick to create and succinct information can be clearly linked where appropriate.

For example:

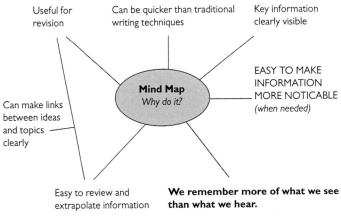

Useful for revision

Can be quicker than traditional writing techniques

Key information clearly visible

Can make links between ideas and topics clearly

Mind Map
Why do it?

EASY TO MAKE INFORMATION MORE NOTICABLE
(when needed)

Easy to review and extrapolate information

We remember more of what we see than what we hear.

We remember more of what we do, see and hear than the aforesaid.

I would advise those reading this guide to complete the VARK test by Neil Fleming which can be easily found by doing a quick internet search. If you find yourself to be a visual learner, use the Mapping Method. If you find yourself to be an auditory learning, ask to record the lecture or workshop and use whichever simple note making method you prefer. (Never record your lecturers secretly as this is rude.) Additionally, you may find that your university has a VLE (virtual learning environment) which includes several lecture recordings.

If you find you are a learner who prefers reading input, attempt to use the Solid Block Writing Method (only if you can touch type), otherwise use the outline method or some combination of the two. Finally, if you are a kinaesthetic learner, use the Mapping Method and attempt to recreate this from memory using Post-Its or consider locus learning when editing your revision notes; locus learning is when you revise a particular topic in a given (exclusive) location. For example, only revise topic a, in room 1, topic b, in room 2 etc. This has been proven, in some cases, to aid memory.

Extensive methods
CORNELL METHOD

The Cornell Method was created by Walter Pauk and was named after the institution he worked for: Cornell University. It is a combination of trigger words, a note making method of the student's choosing and short summary. In my opinion, it is a fantastic way of making notes that is applicable to most subjects.

To follow this method, you need to divide your A4 page into three sections, by drawing three lines in an 'I' shape; one vertical about 1-2 inches from the left of the page, two horizontal about 2 inches from the bottom and top of the page.

Section A   points/terms/names etc, to be explained
                   in Section B.

(Lower end of Bloom's taxonomy – that which you will rote learn).

Section B   a method of your choosing

*(I use the Outline Method here – choose one after completing
the VARK test).*

Section C   summary of notes (try to keep it short).

(think of this as a header section).

For example:

Section A	Section B

Mohammed	Muslims believe Mohammed to be the final prophet.
	    He was a trader and unable to read or write.
	        Yet, he united the Arab tribes, founded a major religion and created an empire.

Hadith	Stories about Mohammed not in the Qu'ran. Isnad (authority of an individual Hadith).
Qu'ran	Qu'ran means recital. Kitab means book.. Today's Qu'ran was not collated until after Mohammed's death (time of the 3rd Caliph)

Section C   Important influences in Islam

I have included a version of the Cornell Note Making paper (both lined and blank) that I use at Heythrop College for reference in order to make the above clearer. I also include later the Heythrop Method note making paper, which you can photocopy for your own personal use.

Cornell Method pauk	Subject:	Date Class
Facts/Dates/ Names/Places etc.	Notes	

Summary

Cornell Method pauk	Subject:	Date
		Class

Facts/Dates/ Names/Places etc.	Notes
Summary	

The advantage of using the Cornell Method is that you can change Section B into any *simple note making method* you like. It is also universal across subjects, as far as note making methods go. I have used the Outline Method (see page 70), however, you could just as easily insert a mind map if you prefer in section B. Section C provides clarity for revision and section A, a sequence of trigger words that stem from Section C.

HEYTHROP METHOD

I created the Heythrop Method in 2013 because I felt that there wasn't a note-making method which specifically suited philosophy or theology students. Such students need to be able to compartmentalise arguments and theories as well as have strengths and weaknesses readily viewable.

To follow this method, you need to divide your page into three sections by drawing two horizontal lines across the page evenly spaced. Then, add a shorter horizontal title line to the top left of each newly created section and a shorter vertical line towards the right of each section. When using this method, only write on one side of the A4 paper. This is because you can later cut your A4 pages and turn the segments into revision cards, without the need to heavily edit the pages; instead, you

Heythrop Method	Subject:	Date
		Class

Strengths/Weaknesses

Strengths/Weaknesses

Strengths/Weaknesses

will need only to arrange your cut-outs. That is, to put each piece of paper into an appropriate container with a relevant title so you can later revise from it.

For example:

Inductive Arguments

	+	-
Russell's Turkey	N/A	An assumption that the past will dictate future events.
Every day a turkey is fed at 6am. The Turkey believes the same will happen tomorrow. One Christmas day at 6am the turkey's head is chopped off!		

The advantage of using the Heythrop Method is that it creates segments of arguments which can be presented in such a way that enables straightforward revision as aforementioned. Also, like the Cornell Method, the larger section can make use of any of the simpler note making methods of the student's choosing. In addition, the + and – (strengths and weaknesses) present the information as it is presented by the lecturer; that is, either supporting or highlighting weaknesses of a view. The latter is particularly useful if you are trying to identify the *spectrum of thought* within a topic. Something philosophers and theologians must do if they are to understand their disciplines holistically. That is, where a particular view/theory is situated within a *spectrum*. The top left shorter horizontal line serves to highlight trigger words.

Whichever method you choose to use, either complex or simple, it is important that you prepare yourself before you enter the lecture hall. You should ensure you have read the lecture reading before attending class and have with you:

- Highlighters
- Pens & additional ink
- Paper (if required)

With these complex methods, it is further useful if you prepare your pages with the line divisions prior to the lecture.

On the following page I also provide a second example of the Heythrop Method, for those with larger writing.

Heythrop Method	Subject:	Date
		Class

	Strengths/Weaknesses

	Strengths/Weaknesses

Time Management

Arnold Bennett wrote an interesting book in the early 20th century called *How to Live on 24 Hours a Day*. It is a little dated now, nevertheless, it contains many excellent tips that are transferable to students studying in higher education. The book is viewable online (for free) using Google Books. If you prefer to read a hard copy, there are newer editions which you can purchase.

A good task that can be derived from this book is to create a written table of activities that you have completed during the day broken down into intervals of activity and time spent doing 'x'. Some tutors suggest that you divide your day into 15 minute intervals, others an hour. I opted for 30 minutes, as the more frequent the readings the more effective your table will prove to be, but equally I acknowledge the tedious nature of creating such a table; every 30 minutes is about all I could handle when I completed this for myself.

Adapt the timeframe as you feel you are able. However, never less than an hour interval. After several days you will quickly see what you spend most of your time doing during the week and would then be able to develop structured strategies to help you manage your commitments and eliminate procrastination.

Using this method, one of my students once identified that he was spending 10+ hours a week playing video games. He was surprised at the length of time devoted to this and gave his games console away during the exam period to eliminate this distraction.

To complete the following table effectively, you can either set a 30 minute countdown timer using your mobile (or an egg timer, if you want to be a little more egg-centric) and write down what you did in that time interval when the timer reaches zero (remember to turn it off when you go to sleep). Or instead, every time you change task, write down what you have done, rounding up the time to the nearest half hour.

It is important that you do not try to alter your usual routine because you are keeping a record as this would only deter from the effectiveness of the exercise.

Remember to include all tasks: cooking, travel & social, etc. This is something you could take to your personal or study skills tutor at university who would then be able to give you some specific tips to help improve your study effectiveness based on your usual daily routines.

For example, a student who is usually traveling for long periods of time, I would suggest reading an article on the train/bus (if there were few changes). If there were many changes, or reading on a train makes you dizzy, I would suggest downloading a text to speak programme so that you could play the text through headphones while you travel. This way, you could get through hours more reading a week than you would otherwise.

I provide a copy of the aforementioned exercise on the next page for your personal use which has been inspired by Bennett's work and which I have used previously in my seminars.

Inspired by **Arnold Bennett**: *'How to live on 24 Hours'*

A time recording log

Date:

Time (30 minute intervals)	Activity	Can this be altered?		If Y/N why?	
		Y	N		
		Y	N		
		Y	N		
		Y	N		
		Y	N		
		Y	N		
		Y	N		
		Y	N		
		Y	N		
		Y	N		

Time (30 minute intervals)	Activity	Can this be altered?		If Y/N why?
		Y	N	
		Y	N	
		Y	N	
		Y	N	
		Y	N	
		Y	N	
		Y	N	
		Y	N	
		Y	N	
		Y	N	

Ask Yourself:

Can you find 90 minutes a day? Could you find more? What are the activities that take up the most amount of your time?

How do I prepare for my exam?

Not all universities have exams at the end of the academic year; Oxford Brooks, for example, offers courses that are entirely coursework based. However, this is the exception rather than the norm. Therefore, most students will need to understand the essential elements of exam preparation in order to maximise their potential during what can be a stressful period. Additionally, if your university does not assess you using exams, you can still use the tips in this section for coursework effectively with some adaptation.

There are some students who perform well in their coursework, but underachieve in an examination. There are many reasons for this, but fundamentally they all stem from the same core reason: adequate preparation. In this section, we will address the questions *when* and *how* you should start preparing.

I have chosen to keep this section as short as possible. Believe me, you do not want to spend too much time reading about 'how to revise'. You ought to be revising! Therefore, I have broken the process down into three simple steps:

Get hold of past exam papers

There is a vast selection of past papers which are usually kept in onsite libraries or on the VLE in most universities. Ensure you access these.

Past exam papers are an extremely valuable resource. They give you an opportunity to practise writing a model answer within the allocated time; they are an important part of your preparation. If you have not spent any time writing answers to past exam questions, you will underachieve. In addition, studying the questions that have been previously asked in the last 3-5 years gives you a good potential guide as to what may be asked in the examination. You can then use this to predict, to some extent, what will come up but do so with caution.

It is important to ensure that you do not 'bury all your eggs in one basket'. Be sure to revise adequate material to ensure that even if your predictions are inaccurate, you will be guaranteed a question on a topic that you have revised. To this end, it is a good idea to regularly practise writing a variety of exam-style essays so that, when you sit the exam, you are well prepared. Use your lecture notes, formulate study groups and use the reading lists provided in your respective modules to help you in this process. Try to spend time thinking about the past questions you find, so that when you are in the exam, you are not spending time thinking, but instead writing what you have pre-thought (of course, after a short plan; this aids recollection).

This is particularly pertinent for philosophy and theology students, as in such examinations across many universities, entrance exams and exam-boards throughout the country, multiple questions are presented which the student can then select from. You will seldom have to answer everything.

Revise effectively

It is important to revise effectively in the period before your examination. So much so that it is not too early to start revising as much as four months before an exam date. This is so that you familiarise yourself with the respective theorists. Use a revision style that compliments your note making method. (See Additional Tips on Time Management). In fact, at university, there should be a regular study habit that is adopted from the beginning of the academic year. Every day should incorporate some time towards recapping learnt materials; remember, Edgar Dale said we remember things better if we repeat them within two weeks.

Know what to look for in exams

An exam question set will seldom ask you to expound all your knowledge. Instead, it will ask you a selective question within the boundaries of your studies. Thus, be sure to understand key words and themes associated with your area of study. You must understand both what to present and, likewise, what not to present.

In many cases, pre-university marks are awarded in a manner that is called 'positive marking'. This is when the examiner looks for points, usually from pre-set lists, which are expected to be found in an exam answer. The examiner is then able to award marks when these points are presented. Revising for the exam, with this approach in mind, while it can work in elementary levels at university, is not wholly adequate. Instead, negative marking is applied at university. This means marks can be lost for unclear and/or contradicting arguments. Therefore, you must have a deeper understanding of the material and be able to critically analyse the respective question without contradicting yourself.

Additionally, you might find it useful to practise recognising those restrictive, directive and topical terms within exam questions (see page 24). You can do this effectively using past papers.

Ask yourself

Have you double checked:
- The **date** & **time** of the exam.
- The **location**. (If this is unfamiliar, visit the centre beforehand to ensure that you do not get lost on the day!).
- The **length** of the exam.

In the exam:
- Read the instructions with great care. Here, it will stipulate how many questions you will need to answer. If you are asked to answer three questions, it is better to answer three questions to a good standard, than two excellently and one not at all. *(Consider: if each question is worth 33%, and you only answer two questions, even if you get a 1st (70%) for two of the answered questions, you would be likely to attain 46% overall).*
- Have you highlighted the restrictive words or clauses in red, directions in yellow and key words (topical terms) in green?
- Have you read the questions carefully? Write an answer only on what you have been asked.
- Keep a watch with you in the exam to manage your time. Using past papers, you should already know how many questions you will need to answer. It is best to read the introductory information in the exam in order to double

check in case anything has changed. Work out how much time you have for each answer and stick to it strictly.

- Always carry spare pens/inks.
- Spend a moment thinking about the question, write a short plan and then get down to answering the question. Do not spend too long contemplating; this is particularly tempting for philosophers and theologians.
- Leave several lines between each exam question; in the event you finish early and want to return to a previous question to add something to a conclusion, this space will prove useful.
- Do cross out work that you do not want marked, but do not scribble it out; it may still be considered.

It is extremely tempting to dive into answering the question when the exam supervisors say, "You can now begin writing". However, take a moment to digest the question. It is good practice to write a short plan before beginning, so that you have ordered your ideas.

If revision has been done correctly, this will be remembering what you have pre-thought and those exam essays that you have pre-written, selecting the relevant information and making a brief note of the said information before you begin writing your essay. It is important to do this so that you remember to stay on target in the exam. Constantly ask yourself, 'am I answering the question'?

Revision Tips in Light of Note Making Methods

The Cornell Method:

Your Page:

Column 1	**Column 2**
Key Words	Definition
Dates	Ideas
Terms	Notes
Questions	
Summary	

Write the information in column 1 on separate cards and then, on the reverse, copy the body of relevant notes. Keep the cards you create to one side and, once completed, place these in a plastic wallet or other such container. Label each container accordingly with the summary at the end of your page. Repeat the process as needed to create a number of cards which would be contained in different plastic wallets/containers. You can then allocate several hours to revising each area of study.

Solid-block Writing:

Your Page:

```
                          Text
```

With a yellow/orange highlighter, highlight the main terms, key words and other important information. If you have touch-typed the text, print it off so that you can do this – don't simply do it on the screen. Once you have done this, copy these words onto a separate A4 sheet in a list format. Using the words on this list, try and recall information from your solid-block text. Re-write this on a separate A4 page, and see how much of the original text you were able to remember. Repeat the process until you are able to remember all of the information. You can keep a *mark out of 10* which will indicate how well you understood and were able to remember the original information. Then, identify areas which need development (from your *marking out of 10*) and focus on those.

Take care to not do this on a simply superficial level. Dr Stephen Chew showed that it is only at the higher level of processing where revision is most effective. Therefore, simply trying to learn the terms as single isolated facts will not help you in creating a coherent revision plan or aid any form of meaningful retention for that matter. Instead, a good idea here would be to consider 'how would you deal with x', 'was there ever a time in your life where you experienced y' etc... If you find this difficult to postulate, ask yourself specifically:

- How would I react to my brother/sister saying s/he has had a conversion experience? (Principle of Credulity).
- If I were faced with evil, would this affect any faith perspective I had? Why? (Problem of Evil).
- How did/would I react to seeing a beautiful sunrise/natural event? (Numinous Experience).

Fundamentally, engaging with the lower ends of Bloom's taxonomy in a personal manner naturally leads you to application, analysis and evaluation. Finally, it helps engrain information into already existing frameworks.

Mind Mapping Method:

Your Page:

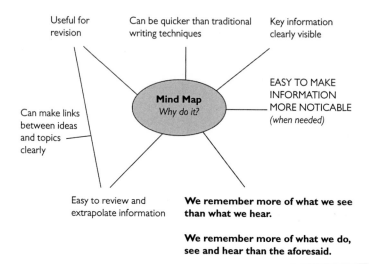

Spend 30 seconds looking at your mind-map then, put it to one side and try to recreate it as accurately as possible on a separate A4 page. Take as long as needed to do this, or until you run out of ideas then check to see if your knowledge matches your lecture notes. Repeat this process until you can recall all the information. You can even measure the amount of time it takes to recreate the mind-map and thus see the positive correlation as you revise if you feel you require a little incentive.

After doing this, always try to link the information on the mind-map back to the topic to which it is relevant. You might want to do this explicitly, e.g. writing how each is related. Or instead, you might want to simply compile the above into different lecture notes/topics so that all the information is easily accessible in one place.

Overview Method:

Your Page:

	(Bloom's Taxonomy)
Main Term	*Knowledge*
Define term	*Understanding*
It's application	*Application*
Analysis	*Analysis*
Strengths and Weaknesses	*Evaluation*

Using flash cards, write the main term on one side and the complete understanding on the other; you can even include an evaluative statement etc. (No more than a short sentence for each card, or you will run out of space). Use these to revise from with the Cornell Method. Alternatively, you can use these to create a mind map or another visual aid.

Remember:

Use the revision method that best suits you and your note writing style. It may be the case that you use several or all of these methods.

Additional Tips on Time Management - revision

It is important to revise effectively in the period before your examinations. It is not unreasonable to spend some time at the end of each topic within a module, revising the material, even if this is many months before the exams. This is because you must make sure that you familiarise yourself with those key thinkers who are relevant to your exams. This can only be done if you effectively manage your time, and with repetition. It is important to build a mental resource of key names and theories as you will not have the usual resources available to you in the exam: chiefly, a library or other textual resources.

How many hours should I set aside for revision?
Students are recommend to put aside 40 hours a week when studying full time for a university degree. (Of course, this is altered for students studying part-time, but not to the same extent: 25 hours a week). This time includes attending lectures, seminars, reading and writing time.

There is some disagreement amongst study skill tutors as to how forthcoming we should be with the above information;

this is because, while a useful recommendation, if not met, it can demoralise students. I believe that you should be given the information and decide how best to proceed for yourself, which is why I include the information above.

Please keep in mind that during the exam period, it is likely that you will no longer have any coursework due. Likewise, the time with your lecturer has probably come to an end. This does not mean, however, that the 40 hour recommendation is now diminished. Instead, it is expected you will spend a greater amount of time in private study, in the library, reading and revising.

Note: During the first week back after the Easter holidays, lecturers may offer you a revision session. Go to this as it will prove invaluable.

Take regular breaks

During your exam revision, it is important that you take regular breaks. The mind is similar, in some metaphorical way, to a muscle. You do not want to burn out before you have dedicated any serious time to revision (ideally you do not want to burn out at all), and likewise you do not want to revise in a superficial manner that will not truly benefit you in the exams. Getting the balance right can be difficult, especially if you have not taken an exam for some time. So remember to take regular breaks (including snacking) and break up reading/writing tasks with other activities while revising.

Examples of 'one cycle' of revision:

20	10	20	10	20	10	20	10
Revise	Break	Revise	Break	Revise	Break	Revise	Break

or

25	5	25	5	25	5	25	5
Revise	Break	Revise	Break	Revise	Break	Revise	Break

or

30	15	30	15	30	15	30	15
Revise	Break	Revise	Break	Revise	Break	Revise	Break

Seldom can the mind concentrate and effectively absorb information for more than 30 minute periods. Some students lock themselves away and try revising without a break. This will work well for a short while, but mental fatigue will soon take hold; you must make time for regular breaks.

What counts as:

A break:	A short walk
	Play some music
	Have a snack
	Short* chat with a friend
Revision:	Reading a passage and making notes on it
	Writing/remembering revision cards
	Making a mind-map
	Discussion group with friends**
	Practise writing past questions***
	Making bullet-points on topics
	Reviewing your lecture notes

* Take care not to overrun into your revision time!

** Take care when revising with others. Sometimes it can be very effective, while at other times it can become fruitless. Do not be embarrassed if you decide to leave a group if the discussion time becomes '*who tweeted what/when*', etc. Kindly excuse yourself and continue your work elsewhere.

*** When writing past questions, stick to the time that is allocated under exam conditions and do not follow the cycles of revision, as this would create an unrealistic experience.

Remember:

Those who say "I didn't revise" probably did, and just don't want to admit it. If they really didn't you may notice that they are missing next year.

Your revision should be active as far as possible; you remember far more of what you learn actively rather than passively. The list of revision techniques above is geared towards active learning methods, rather than passive ones. Adapt the list as you feel appropriate and what you find works best for you and ask yourself personal questions surrounding the revision materials to create and encourage higher level processing.

Create a Plan
Work out the number of days until your exam. Ensure you create a plan which will allow you enough time to revise all the materials comfortably. Allocate several hours to each module per day and systematically work through your materials. If you decide to work in this way, use the first example as this will allow you to cover each module using *one cycle* per day. Alternatively, create your own system if you feel this would work better for you. What is important is that you regularly change your revision task

(i.e. by using various learning methods) and remember to take regular breaks.

If you completed the VARK test, or already know what type of learner you are, i.e. what learning medium works best for you, then try to use revision tasks that are compatible with your learning style. Remember to change the tasks to make each revision slot most effective.

On the next pages I provide an example of a revision plan. You may wish to recreate something like this up to 4 months before your exam dates. The example overleaf is only based on approximately one month's revision, and does not include days off, which you might want to factor in. However, it serves its purpose as a basic illustration. Under each topic, you will find a number which is how confident the student is regarding that subject which affects the choice of letter: each letter is given an amount of time in a day, A being the most and E the least. You would have as many letters as topics.

Trinity	Jesus	Scripture	Modernity	Eucharist	Theology	Ethics & Morality	
8	8	2	5	7	5	2	
C		A	B	D			21 July
	C	A	D		B		22
C			B	D		A	23
	C	D			B	A	24
C		A	B			D	25
	C		D	A	B		26
C		D	B			A	27
	C			D	B	A	28
C		A	D			B	29
	C	A	B	D			30
C		B	D	A	B		31
	C		B	D		A	1 Aug
C		A		B	D		2
	C	A	D			B	3
C				A,B		D	4
	C	B	D	A			5
				Exam			6
B	C				D, E	A	7
A		E	D		B	C	8
C, E	D					A, B	9
Exam						Exam	10
	A	C	D		B, E		11
	Exam				Exam		12
		A, C, E	B, D				13
		Exam	Exam				14

Time	Revision Tasks	Notes
8 – 9	Breakfast	
9 – 9.30	A	Make mind maps Topics 1/2.
9.40 – 10.10	B	Discussion group skype.
10.20 – 10.50	C	
11 – 11.30	D	
11.40 – 12.10	E	
12.20 – 12.50	F	
12.50 – 2pm	Lunch	
2 – 2.30	A	Recall mind maps. Topic 1. Re-do Topic 2
2.40 – 3.10	B	
3.20 – 3.50	C	
4 – 4.30	D	
4.40 – 5	E	Make plan for Practice Paper
5 – 6.15pm	Practise completing a paper	
6.30 – 7	A	Recall mind maps. Topic 2
7.10 – 7.40	B	
7.50 – 8.20	C	
8.30 – 9	A	
9pm	Dinner/rest	

Active Learning Vs Passive Learning; metacognitive frameworks

However you choose to revise, you will be far more effective if you learn explicitly rather than implicitly. Ask yourself, can you articulate specifically how a piece of information is relevant to the topic? If you can, it is likely that you understand the information well. If not, additional effort is required. By being able to articulate relevance, you will be more likely to remember the information, as placing it on an existing framework of knowledge is more effective in revision terms than simply trying to learn isolated facts as aforementioned.

It is my hope that this short guide has given you several tips on how to approach your academic studies at university and has inspired you in a small way to take your studies seriously, passionately and with an academic mind. Genuinely, you can achieve so much, if you put in the work.

I will now leave you with another one of my favourite teachers of pedagogy: Dr Chew. He currently has several excellent videos online (YouTube) which address study skills specifically and which are from the perspective of an academic Dr, rather than that of an academic study skills tutor, (in all comparisons,

I would prefer the former). Please watch these videos and also familiarise yourself with: B. Bloom, E. Dale & N. Fleming at least, as the work of these excellent educators are taught in the PGCE (Post Graduate Certificate in Education) which aims to teach prospective teachers how to teach most effectively. I mention this because, at university, you become a teacher of yourself, and, hopefully, learn to learn independently. Having such a skill will help you go far in whatever you choose to do after attaining your degree.

As a final nugget of wisdom, please become familiar with Thomas Hyde and James Jenkins' experiment in 1969, which was a collaboration between the University of Minnesota & Case Western Reserve University; ask yourself, which of the categories do you feel you fit in? Dr Chew's aforementioned videos will direct you to this.

Answers Page

What are the Jewish responses to the Holocaust?

'All ethical statements are meaningless' Discuss with reference to at least two theorists.

Examine the ways in which an ontological argument can be used to prove or disprove the existence of God.

Is Virtue Ethics a subjective or objective ethical theory?

What was the achievement of Chalcedon?

Nine Dot Problem - solution

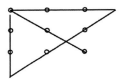

Have you ever heard of the phrase: 'Think outside of the box', it is likely that this is where the phrase originated from and is now used to encourage individuals to approach problems from non-conventional means, that is 'outside of the box', which is often how we find answers to some of the puzzles that we are presented with. If you are a tutor using this example, don't say "Think outside of the box", as this usually gives the game away before you can sufficiently perplex students with the puzzle which, in the very act, makes the lesson objective all the more memorable.

ND - #0030 - 060921 - C0 - 203/133/5 - PB - 9781909644878 - Gloss Lamination